The Coming of A New
Dawn

7/29/08

To Elisa,

Thank you for all your positive
energy. I really appreciate
you.

Dawn

The Coming of A New *Dawn*

✦

A book of inspirational thoughts

Dawn A. Bruce

iUniverse, Inc.
New York Lincoln Shanghai

The Coming of A New *Dawn*
A book of inspirational thoughts

iUniverse books may be ordered through booksellers or by contacting:

iUniverse
2021 Pine Lake Road, Suite 100
Lincoln, NE 68512
www.iuniverse.com
1-800-Authors (1-800-288-4677)

ISBN: 978-0-595-47188-1 (pbk)
ISBN: 978-0-595-91467-8 (ebk)

Printed in the United States of America

Special thanks to
Dr. Emil Moxey
for his time and patience in editing this book.

This book is dedicated to my son who has been and continues to be a wonderful blessing in my life.

Contents

FOREWORD

This book was written to encourage all those who are experiencing change within. These writings are from personal thoughts that have come to me over the years, as I journey on my path to self-enlightenment. Some thoughts are just one-line and some are expanded musings. I also use the terms God, Universe, Creator and Spirit interchangeably. In putting this book together I soon realized that there is more to life than what we see initially. At times a still small voice or a very strong and forceful voice declares that there is so much more for you. As you journey on your path to enlightenment, which is all about knowing yourself, allow the Universe to lead you to wonderful places where you have never been before. I pray that these thoughts will speak to you in a way that will bring forth healing and move you along your personal path.

Peace & Blessings

Dawn

HEALING AND LETTING GO

*It's over now. Experiences help us to grow and see
what's going on in our lives, our fears, beauty, strengths, gifts, and where we
are right now.*

HEALING AND LETTING GO

Isn't it time to get rid of the souvenirs that we've collected from the events in our lives? You know, those souvenirs that remind us of what we did, when we did it, how we did it, and whom we did it to? They pile up and accumulate in the places within us that need the space so that we can heal. Go into those hidden places, pull out those souvenirs, and get rid of them. They are worthless. Destroy them; remove the remains and let your path be clear.

When an explosion (those things that come and turn our lives upside down) occurs, every reason and excuse gets blown up and we can't escape. There are no more excuses to hold on to. The old is gone and the opportunity is here for us to heal and let go of whatever we don't need on our journey. Don't resist the inevitable, which is change. Everything must change in order to grow.

Sometimes experiences can leave a bad taste in our mouths. This taste lingers and seems at times difficult to get rid of. It can affect us to the point where everything tastes terrible. We can brush and rinse with the truth for fresh breath, so when we speak, our mouths will utter words of life and wisdom from our experiences. As we heal we kill the germs (the lies others told us and we told ourselves) and let go of the pain that would cause decay.

Why be tied up in a straight jacket that society, other people, and fear have tried to put on us? We don't have to be tied up any longer. Why continue to use medication from someone else's formula for life? Is it working for you? If not, let it go and let the Universe show you the way.

Why do we keep visiting the haunted house of old memories that constantly haunt and torment us? The house has been shut down; it's in the past. Stop paying for a ride that leaves you unhappy and frustrated. Yes, we'll still feel and remember all that has happened. Sometimes we might think nothing is changing because we still remember the past, but calm down, start breathing and let the answers that are needed come to you.

♥

The season is over, so take the mistletoe down along with the other decorations. Don't pack them away but throw them out. Life has a way of showing us that there is a time to put away, let go of, and bury the old in order to embrace the new. Sometimes we want to hold on to all the old decorations from celebrations, different events, and gatherings. Sometimes these experiences leave long lasting marks in our lives. There may be a tendency to hang the mistletoe for Christmas and when we come into contact with the images of what happened we kiss these experiences and remember the pain. Old, outdated decorations must be thrown out so that we can heal and create something new.

♥

Energy wants to flow through and move in our lives. This flow represents growth and progress, not emptiness. Sometimes there are stop signs and traffic cops (rigid and inflexible ways) that need to be removed. The traffic cops give tickets for any and everything that we feel is a violation. They are on every corner along with stop signs. Fire the traffic cops and take down all the unnecessary signs. Your traffic lights don't always have to be on red (stop) or yellow (caution) all the time. The Universe wants to flow through us instead of stopping all the time and being ticketed for no reason. Are you trying to control things that you may need to let go of? It's time to go ahead and drive.

♥

It's over now. Experiences help us to grow and see what's going on in our lives, our fears, beauty, strengths, and gifts and where we are right now. Do you look at your life and see how there were times you created situations you didn't want? All of these experiences were opportunities for us to learn worthwhile lessons and do things in new ways.

♥

Right now take responsibility for the situations you created and not beat yourself up nor have regrets, but learn from them. Many times we stop ourselves from moving on. There's a contract we make with ourselves but don't fulfill. Sign on the dotted line where your signature is needed for life to move forward. Release the past, let go, take time for and be good to yourself.

♥

Letting go means not worrying about the outcome of a situation, but going beyond your own understanding and letting it be what it needs to be. The Creator will take care of us. The hardness and pain are leaving, now you are becoming softer, supple, and smooth.

♥

Do you really want to continue going through mug shots to get suspects (family, co-workers, classmates, old girlfriends, boyfriends, and the list goes on) for past crimes you feel have been committed in your life? It's over now. Stop issuing warrants for their arrests. Use your energy to heal, make changes, and move ahead with your life.

♥

Transcend the garbage. The garbage (feelings that are blocking you) is the leftover of life's experiences that you can't use.

♥

The Universe wants to flush you. Flush not only means using water to wash away but also growth, expansion, and abundance. Stretch out your creativity. It's been balled up too long and needs room to grow and flourish. We have more than we realize.

♥

Unplug from the external and learn to plug into yourself. You have the answers inside of you. Be still so you can hear what they are. There are different types of plugs, low self-esteem, insecurity, anger, fear, and many more. Some people run on outside energy when they can plug into and tap into themselves. The sources you may have plugged into don't have enough voltage to keep you going. When you put different plugs into someone or something else you can burn a fuse. That person or thing can burn a fuse on you. Your energy will come from within.

♥

At times when we are experiencing challenges in our lives, we sometimes have the tendency to want to control the outcome of whatever is happening. One day Spirit said to me, "If you want to take matters into your own hands, I'll step back, but if you want Me to take care of the situations in your life, you need to relax." Sometimes this is like a tug of war because I want to hold on but when I let go and stop trying to fix everything on my own, there is more clarity, peace, and the answers are obvious.

There are many situations in my life where I'm learning that I can't deal with them head on (being aggressive, fighting, fearful, or blaming others). There are situations I'll have to address from another angle—handling them not with emotion but with internal guidance. In other words when I'm still and step away from the people, places, and things and speak to the situations using affirmations, that which I was fussing over and getting bent out of shape about start to change because I start to change. This doesn't always happen immediately but I've noticed that it does happen. Divine intuition shows me the answers and I know just what to do.

♥

It's easy to say let it go but it's another thing to actually do it, especially when we seem to want to hold on. We may fight, wrestle, clinch, cry, and grasp people, places, relationships and experiences that are either over or weren't meant to be. Healing starts to take place when we acknowledge it's over, whatever it is.

♥

Leftovers

In my quiet time alone Spirit said you are holding onto leftovers. The leftovers were past experiences that needed to happen so that I could evolve but held on to longer than I was supposed to. My mind kept going over things that were over a long time ago. All that was required was to learn the lesson, love myself, and move on. Instead of doing that the leftovers were kept in the refrigerator and began to form mold and bacteria that after a while caused illness. There was vomiting and diarrhea from the words and thoughts that flowed through me. Now it was time for cleansing by getting rid of the old and allowing the new to flow through me.

♥

Cough Drop

I noticed that in my life there was a constant cough that I was trying to get rid of. It wasn't a physical cough but a spiritual cough. Coughing is a sign that the body wants to get something out, releasing a blockage in the throat. Spirit was showing me that I had to release the greatness that was placed inside of me but I decided to take cough drops. My cough drops were fear, hesitation, and hiding. By sucking on the drops long enough the cough would be suppressed and I could continue on my way and not be bothered. The interesting thing about my cough was that it wouldn't go away no matter how many drops I took. The cough became louder and harsher because I wasn't saying what needed to be said. Spirit wanted me to speak words of peace and encouragement first to myself. It was easy to say it to others but not so easy when it came to me. Spirit wanted me to stop taking the cough drops because the activity of the cough was bringing about necessary changes. These changes were needed to propel my life forward.

♥

Someone Is Sleeping In My Bed

Sometimes we go to bed with people that are not physically in our room. How do we do this? By not letting go of people that we have no control over. We even go to bed with our children by worrying about them. I'm not saying this is easy but it crowds our minds when we take so many people to bed with us. Bosses, co-workers, families, friends, strangers and a host of people we encounter during the day do not need to sleep with us at night. This is something we must continuously practice because it's not hard to be bombarded by people. Think about it, do you really want all of those people in your bed every night? People will leave when we let go of them.

♥

Static Cling

The Universe helped me to see that I had static cling by attracting people and situations that didn't affirm my greatness. When too much energy is focused in one area an attraction develops and people and situations start to appear. In order for us to attract what we want our energy must be focused on loving ourselves and what we really want instead of what we don't want.

♥

Disposable Waste

Many times we go through life with many things happening to us. People say to forget about it, it's water under the bridge. It's not always easy to forget about it. The people and events that happen have been used and must be disposed of properly. It's like waste from hospitals and chemical plants. You just can't throw it out you must wrap it up or do what needs to be done to dispose of it properly.

Many people dump waste illegally and there's poison from the waste or objects such as needles that pollute and contaminate other people and drinking water. Illegal dumping is done when we want to place blame on others and suppress what we have gone through (get this waste off the premises of your mind, body, and spirit.) We must dispose of it properly by releasing, admitting the truth, and forgiving. The people and situations have been used and the material is hazardous (there's a risk involved in getting infected and not growing) after the initial use. We must dispose of the past properly. Waste that is kept contaminates your atmosphere. When waste isn't disposed of correctly it infects not only yourself but also others around you.

♥

Graffiti

When we unconsciously hold onto words that have been said to us and don't let them go, those words are like graffiti that have been sprayed on us. It defaces and vandalizes our property (our self esteem.) Spirit washes away the graffiti. It wasn't painted over because the damage would still be underneath. It has been washed off and any needed repairs and restoration are being done right now.

DEALING WITH CHANGE

Don't be afraid of change.

DEALING WITH CHANGE

One of the most life changing experiences I've ever had was to feel birth and death at the same time. In one week my husband died and four days later my son was born. Talk about turning my world upside down. **_Everything_** changed—my finances, employment, relationships and view of life changed. In my mind I didn't see how I was going to raise my son by myself. I recall crying and telling someone I can't do this. She gently said to me, yes you can do this. Another friend told me to take it one moment at a time.

My husband's death was the catalyst used to get my life moving in another direction. Prior to this experience I knew something wasn't right in my life because I wasn't satisfied. There was more to life and I didn't know how to access it and on another level didn't believe I deserved it. The Universe helped me to see that my husband and his death represented the old that needed to be buried and my son's birth represented newness of life.

A newness of life that helped me to look at myself as the Universe sees me and begin the process of deep healing. A process that was often lonely but necessary. A process that brought out areas that were buried for years and that needed to be uncovered.

♥

Change is inevitable we just can't avoid it. Our bodies, circumstances, relationships, children, friends and much more change all the time. At some point we have to know when certain people, places, and things no longer serve our best interests. We don't have to be afraid of change. Sometimes you may want to go back to the old ways because they're comfortable and you know what to expect. Change can be scary at times especially when you don't know what's going to happen next. The more you let go, the more you will begin to see it is safe to grow up and live life to the fullest.

♥

Are you happy and at peace with yourself? This is a question that isn't asked too often. There are so many distractions coming at us everyday that we don't get a chance just to speak to ourselves and really look at what's happening in our lives. So many people think they are happy with things outside of themselves but if happiness isn't springing from the well within you, it's difficult for anything external to make you happy and at peace internally. Can you stand to be alone with yourself and have an open discussion about what's really happening in your life? If not then this is clearly an opportunity to change.

♥

Pain, the thing we don't want to deal with and try to avoid at all costs but can't escape. What makes pain so difficult to deal with? It hurts and it's not easy to let go of. It causes us to remember when it occurred and who was involved. Pain is also a great teacher. A teacher that gives us the opportunities to learn valuable lessons through personal experiences and make necessary changes.

♥

Buried Alive

Many times we experience situations that makes us avoid or want to forget. The problem is that these issues don't go away but we try to make them go away by burying them alive. We try to kill the living organism (the truth) when it shouldn't die. We also try to resuscitate, give shock treatments, and put on life support that which should be dead (the past). Burying ourselves in the external won't help us to deal with facing the reality that we can't escape. It is time to change. That which is buried wants to get out and come to the surface for air. There is no way we can hide. The truth will always dig us out of the grave that we put ourselves into.

♥

What Do You When The Lights Go Out?

Life has a way of presenting experiences that will shock us. It's like the lights going out all around. Maybe a fuse was blown, light bulb needs changing, or there's a major blackout. When these types of experiences occur the light from within is needed to guide us through the darkness. This light is our intuition. Light helps us to see what we may not have seen before. Why do these things happen? They are opportunities for us to change. In the dark we were tripping over things that needed to be thrown out. The dark can be very frightening for many people because you just can't see where you're going. The beauty of the internal light is that we are responsible for turning it on by listening and following through with the answers that come to us. Sometimes we don't understand the answers but as we live from day to day the darkness begins to leave and the light dominates our lives.

THE PROCESS OF LIFE

Life is a process that utilizes various experiences and people to help us evolve and become aware of the greatness that resides within us.

THE PROCESS OF LIFE

The events of our lives are perfectly designed to help us grow.

♥

No matter what is happening in your life the Creator will never leave you alone. There are times when we feel like we are alone, but we are going through a process. Get ready for greater things to happen in your life. You don't have to run from it, but embrace it. You deserve the best. There is a process to life and a part of this process is preparation. There is a time to get ready and then launch out into deeper waters in your life, the unknown. Are you ready for the next level?

♥

In this process blockages are being cleared; there is cleansing and renewal within. Sometimes it feels like being pushed through a door and all traces of this door have been erased. You are forced to be honest with yourself in order to move in another direction.

♥

Sample life; there are always lessons to be learned.

♥

When I looked at the situations in my life it wasn't easy to trust anyone, let alone myself. My lack of faith was like a hair with split ends. I could rely on the Creator for a little while and when it seemed like things weren't moving fast enough I would lean to my own understanding. I was dried out. Faith is like a moisturizer and when I used it the Spirit helped me not to break off, but to trust the process of life.

♥

Whether I wanted to accept it or not I have a destiny and purpose to fulfill and so do you. We will go through different experiences to get to our ultimate purpose. We are in a growth process.

♥

We are like plants and therefore, in order for plants to grow they need air, water, and sunlight. There are times that fertilizer is needed to help plants to grow. Being fertile is opening up to all the wonderful possibilities for development. Many times we feel that not experiencing difficulties or problems will make our lives easy and that's it. If your life is easy, how will you grow and know what you can or can't do? All of our experiences are like fertilizer so that we can develop what has been placed inside each of us.

♥

It doesn't matter who you are or what you've been through; this doesn't interfere with you being special and having unique qualities. It's all right that there are areas in your life that need improvement and healing, but you're still here for a purpose. If you didn't go through what you went through how would you know how strong you are, or that you didn't need people the way you thought you did? Growth is a process.

♥

Don't allow what seems to be the right thing to do to interfere with what you hear on the inside. You may feel anxious because you are breaking away from what has been the "norm" and learning to follow how the Universe speaks to you. Make the necessary adjustments and go on this wonderful journey.

Life truly is a process; one that has steps in sequence, order, and calls for repetition.

♥

Fresh Squeezed Orange Juice

When I look at my life I think about an orange. In order to extract the juice the orange must be squeezed. Pressure had to be exerted on all sides to bring out the real strength that I didn't know I possessed. Actually, I did know I had the power but was afraid to look at it, let alone use it. The Universe helped me along the way by allowing situations and people to squeeze out the juice, seeds, and pits. The juice possesses the qualities of my being. It's something that has strength and power. The seeds are gifts and talents that have great potential. Pits also come out in the squeezing process and are there for a purpose. They remind me that there are areas in my life that are in the process of developing and maturing.

We are squeezed at different times in our lives to learn valuable lessons and bring out our greatness. Even though the process of being squeezed can be uncomfortable it is necessary for our evolution.

♥

Pickle

One night I heard the Universe say you are in a pickle. A pickle can be a difficult situation or an article of food that has been preserved in brine or in vinegar. I had no idea that being a mother would put me in the pickling process. Transformation takes place as a cucumber turns into a pickle. By having a child I had the opportunity to transform and learn that no matter where I am in life the Universe is there with me. When I feel like I don't have the strength or knowledge to take on the challenges of life, the pickling process reminds me that I'm being preserved and constantly growing. I have the opportunity to be still and know that I can accomplish that, which is set before me.

♥

The Crock-Pot

One day during my quiet time the words crock-pot and slow cook came to me. The crock-pot of life is the preparation process. Being in the crock-pot is helping me to see myself, release what I can't use, and prepare for what's ahead. The crock-pot on slow cook is helping to heal, soften the areas that need more tenderness, and toughen the areas that are too soft. When I go through this process, in the right time and space, the Universe will present me.

♥

The Dark Room

Before digital cameras became so popular people used cameras with film for their pictures. Our lives are like film in a camera. Our experiences are subjects that we take pictures of. In order for others to see our pictures we must go through processing which consists of being developed in a dark room. This is a process that is not always clear to us but since the photographer/Spirit knows what to do we must go through it for our evolution.

When the pictures are ready they can be seen and shared with others. Our experiences are not only for our own benefit but also for the benefit of others. Special effects on the pictures symbolize our gifts and talents. They were in the mind of the photographer and certain experiences brought them out. No one can enjoy pictures unless they are developed. The Universe will take us through the process of being in the dark room so our experiences can be a source of strength in our lives and in the lives of others.

SELF-AWARENESS

Turn on the light and look at yourself! You have a lot of beauty and potential that you don't want to keep hidden in the darkness.

SELF-AWARENESS

We are like dispenser bottles. The dispenser is the heart, and the opening is the mouth. The dispenser reaches to the bottom of the bottle and the contents surround it. Whatever is on the inside will come out. Challenges and difficult people are used to help us dispense what is really inside of us. You know, those areas that aren't readily seen until someone or something comes along to give us a squeeze or push. We know our own ingredients: fear, anger, creativity, love, and the list goes on. Sometimes we may feel that we can hide what's on the inside and no one will recognize us because we are disguised in a nice bottle or package. When you release through your actions and words, you have the opportunity to see yourself. You might ask why am I acting like this? Something is happening, something you need to see. It's time for changes to take place in our lives. Changes for the better are filling you up. I'm still dispensing and this is a continuous process, but I'm also refilling with the right ingredients: peace, love, and clarity. When you let go and dispense you will free yourself.

♥

The more I stay in the dispensing process and release old things; I can see and understand what was in me. I read the fine print, which represents the experiences in my life. There was so much fine print in my life that now I am taking the time to read it thoroughly. To really look at who we are and why we act the way we do, it's important to take the time to read ourselves. I was able to look up the contents one by one and see the effects it had on me. The ingredients had patterns in them. When I read the fine print I found out that I was creating situations myself. One of the great things I discovered was that I could learn new ways to live my life.

♥

It's time to turn on the light and look at ourselves. We have a lot of beauty and potential that we don't want to keep hidden in the darkness.

Unearth the treasures that have been covered up for years by pain, misunderstandings, and fear. The hidden things must come out.

The Universe has taken me inside, turned on the lights, locked the doors, pulled down the shades, and closed the curtains. The potter took the clay and slammed it against the wall. I was made pliable and put on the wheel to be molded into a beautiful vessel.

I was like a keeper at the gate of my life guarding a gold mine. There are so many riches that I only allowed others, including myself, to approach from a distance. There was a 20-foot pole that was shortened a little but not thrown away, because I was still holding on to it. I thought I needed it to keep pain at a distance. This pole kept me from so much. I realize now I don't need the pole and made the choice to destroy it.

Do you ever hear the voice of your gifts calling and your creativity and dreams gently whispering to you? They want to come out but do you keep opening and closing the door to their cries? Open the door. Ignoring them and worrying about how things are going to work out is like a trap door that holds these gifts as hostages. Let the hostages go!

The spell is broken. The truth has been presented and is standing right in front of you. Will you accept it? The only one that can hold you back is yourself.

Are you smuggling from place to place what you have to share with the world? What are you hiding from? Can you really escape yourself? The Universe wants to move you and you want to keep stopping. Why? Are the customs officials (people, places, and things) preventing you from going forward? You have a purpose that will be a blessing to others, so why not share yourself? The Spirit will use you for the right purpose.

After all this time I have finally given the Universe my permission slip for trips to places that I've never heard of or been before. I signed the permission slip when I stopped fighting and let go of the fear. Now I don't have to be stuck in one place. When focusing on how things will, or even can work out, I don't really travel at all. When these areas come together the Universe will arrange all the trips I need to take. I will go places in the areas of finances, relationships, opportunities, fulfilling my destiny, self-appreciation, healthy self-esteem, and love like I've never experienced before. No one else can sign your permission slip but you. Children are given permission slips for trips, which must be signed by parents or guardians, the ones responsible for them. You are responsible for yourself. You are going places so don't carry any bags from the past; you don't need the luggage. Give yourself permission to travel.

When I put the energy of my desires out into the Universe there's a point where I must step back and let the Universe do the rest.

♥

I don't have to worry about details. The Universe is like a secretary that sets up all events and meetings, tells you where to go and what time to be there, makes travel arrangements, screens visitors, and prepares you for everything. The Spirit said all I have to do is follow the leading and show up; the rest is already taken care of.

♥

You must trust yourself. Trust the Universe speaking within you. Stop saying that you don't know because you do know. Stop thinking that you can't because you can.

♥

Be true to yourself. Be still and let the Creator deal with you and speak to you. Don't make any sudden moves. Everyday the Creator is reassuring us that we are not alone. This is a process of getting to know yourself better and falling in love with yourself more and more.

♥

Listen, hear, look, and see. These steps are very important in order to view the big picture of life. Sometimes we do this and become afraid of all that's in front of us. You might wonder if you are hearing or seeing correctly. What's before us may look strange. I've questioned and wanted to understand what was going on, to be sure that this was the way to go. When I learned to trust the Universe within, the external wasn't so strange anymore.

♥

Situations and experiences in life come to unwrap us. Sometimes we don't know what's inside until the cover comes off. Death has unwrapped me. I was like a present, so that when the box was shaken, something was inside but I didn't know what it was. Now, I know.

♥

Experiences have a way of giving us a good pinch or sharp stick so that we will get up. Yes, certain positions are comfortable but when it's time to move and change we can't stay still.

♥

Don't hold back or run for cover. You can do whatever you need to do. The running, hiding, and wanting to avoid experiences won't help you.

Right now accept where you are and learn the lessons from your experiences.

Don't be afraid of yourself. On certain levels you may not want to commit to areas that will build you up because of what may look like inconveniences. All of these inconveniences are preparation for you. Do you know what your assignment in life is? Do you see where you belong? Then it's time to go forth. Why worry about money, a degree, the kids, the spouse, the job and the list goes on? The Universe has everything we need. Know your assignment and carry it out.

We are all spiritual beings that have human experiences. Sometimes human experiences can turn us into a bag lady or bag man. These experiences and the way we dealt with them caused us to be homeless, outside of ourselves, our homes. We are constantly learning new tools to help us as we go from day to day. Sometimes we really don't know how to get out of the situations we're in. We don't always know how to clean off all the dirt, heaviness and the pain, which we carry around for years and years. The decision can be made to change, look at our lives, and take the necessary steps to go back home within us and heal.

<u>*Bag Lady*</u>

I was like a bag lady wandering back and forth down the lonely streets of life. My life was empty, sad, and confused. How did I get this way? I didn't trust myself and went outside to find the answers. When I came back home periodically someone else took over with his or her ideas, convictions, and phobias. I was evicted from my own home, myself. I allowed other people to come in and dispossess me. They moved right in and before I knew it the windows were boarded, the doors locked, and all the lights were out. I tried to get back in but everything was sealed off. I began looking for a place to live but no one wanted me, and most of all I didn't want myself.

I was a homeless young lady carrying around the past. My bags were filled with bruises, pain, shame, and lack of confidence, low self-esteem, and loneliness all from the market of fear. I paid a heavy price for all of this.

My layered clothes were like a shell that I used to protect myself. The dirt on my body smelled and I hid the mess of my mistakes (wrong choices) on me.

I wandered around because I didn't have a home. I looked for shelter from the elements of life that were harsh against me. I didn't know how to clean off the dirt or that I had the power to clean myself off at all.

One day as I walked around I looked at myself in the mirror and realized that underneath all my mistakes, the dirt, layered clothes and everything else I was buried. I started to dig myself out.

I decided to look in my bags and empty them out. It was time to get rid of the pain, shame, low self-esteem, bruises, and lack of confidence. I began to really take a long hard look at myself and make the decision to change. I needed to carry something around but it wasn't going to be the past. I made a trip to the market of life and started to put love, joy, peace, abundance, prosperity, and a renewed mind into myself. I am no longer a wandering bag lady and feel lighter. Now I'm going back home, moving in so that I can live in peace.

♥

"Knock knock. Is anyone home?" Spirit said to me one day, "I constantly ring your bell and knock on the door and sometimes you're not at home. You're outside distracted by what's going on around you. You get blinded by your emotions and you're out gallivanting at a neighbor's house minding someone else's business and not your own. When I knock or ring your bell, listen and answer." The Universe is always speaking, giving guidance, direction, reassurance and whatever is needed. Spirit said, "Don't be side tracked by what's outside of you."

♥

Vacuum Packed

I was like a vacuum-packed item trying to keep myself free from germs (experiences of life). The problem with this is that nothing was going out or coming in. My past pain took the form of additives that caused me to be sealed. My expiration date had passed and I was still out in the open experiencing the very thing I was trying to avoid which was life. The experiences of death gave me the release I needed so that I could live life to the fullest. I learned that it was all right to be exposed. Additives weren't needed but the truth needed to be faced.

♥

Painkillers

When we use painkillers they may give us temporary relief from what we're feeling, but they don't treat the cause of the pain. Pain is a symptom of a much deeper issue. The problem with painkillers is that they are chemicals. We do not know all the side effects they will have on us. In order for healing to take place we must deal with the real problems, not mask them. We can abuse painkillers by taking them excessively and when we no longer get the desired effect, we take more and consequently may become dependent.

Sometimes we become dependent on other people and things to try to escape what we're feeling, but it doesn't go away. We have to deal with it without trying to dull the pain. When feelings come up, identify them and let them come out. Get to the core and heal naturally by going through the process of healing.

♥

Bounty Hunter

I was my own bounty hunter. I posted pictures of myself wherever I went. I was wanted for a crime that I created. Not only did I do the bounty hunting, but I also handled myself in a rough and cruel manner. I brought myself in for questioning. The bail was posted when I told myself that I am going to do better. I jumped bail when it was time for me to deal with things that weren't pleasant. Listening to the laws of others and my own ideas caused me to think that I was charged with a felony. The Creator said that I don't have to run because no crime was committed. You are not wanted. Tear down the posters, release yourself, and live.

♥

When you look in the mirror, what do you see? Take a good look and be honest with yourself. Don't see what you think you should see or what other people think you should see. The reflection in the mirror is you. Do you see someone that you love or someone that is fearful, angry or resistant? Take the time to see yourself. Take the time to see who is in the mirror. Do you love what you see? If not it's time for change.

What are we telling ourselves? What do you tell yourself everyday? I'm smart, stupid, loveable, scared, beautiful or ugly? What we say to ourselves and to the world is either killing or propelling us to move forward. Are we committing suicide with our words or are we using our words to evolve to higher levels. Think about it.

Do we see silhouettes and images of a person but not the person we really are? Sometimes we're cloaked with other people's ideas and our own fears. When we look in the mirror it helps us to see what's really going on.

People are also mirrors and show us many aspects of ourselves whether we like it or not.

♥

All the answers to all the questions we have are already inside of us. Notice that so often you already know what to do and the words of others are mostly confirmations of what we already know.

What do I want? Have you ever asked yourself this question lately? This cannot be answered by anyone else but you. What do you want to do that's been put on hold or forgotten? What makes you peaceful? What talents, gifts, and desires need to come out? What do you need to get rid of or embrace? Have a conversation with yourself to see what's happening in your life.

Dealing with death and birth at the same time made me sit down with myself, by myself, and really look at what was ailing me. Why did this happen and what was going to happen now? This golden opportunity helped me to look through the storage rooms within, unlock doors, open chests, look under beds, and open closets to see what was there. All those memories, cries, and experiences that were suppressed, shoved, and hidden in the deep parts of my being were starting to show themselves. They all had one identity and one name, which was fear.

Life presents opportunities for us to be involved in relationships at home, work, school, or just about anywhere that can be fiery at times. We enter into relationships that put us in the fire to bring up what's really inside and needs to come up. Strength, love, anger, resentment, just about anything can come up. Fire does deep and intense work within so we can learn to shine on the outside.

Open Up Your Treasure Chest

I was like a closed, locked, and bolted treasure chest full of jewels, riches, and valuables. The pain from the past caused me to hide from myself. Fear caused me to be tightly sealed and put under lock and key. I decided to bury myself under the dirt of life's experiences. In order to open up my treasure chest I had to admit that I was in pain that went as far back as I could remember. Despite what happened I was not a horrible person. My travel to uncover what was locked away was a journey that took time and patience with myself. Diving deep and recovering my treasure chest, cleaning it off, destroying the lock and looking inside, gave me the opportunity to actually touch my jewels. This has taught me to value myself. Some of my jewels were a little tarnished, scratched, and dented but they were still priceless. The Universe used every experience and every person as a lock opener to help me open up and share what was hidden.

Come Out, Come Out, You Know Where You Are

One day I heard Spirit say, "Come Out, Come Out, You Know Where You Are?" Hearing this made me look at my life and start the process of looking at myself. Too often I played hide and seek with myself. Spirit said you know exactly where you are. You know that you're looking for yourself on the external when what you must look at is internal. In order to know myself I had to go inside and come back out. Confronting myself was necessary to make the changes that were needed. There was a part of me that knew something wasn't right and deserved something better. I knew I had the ability to make changes but decided to hide. I learned not to be afraid of myself. I had to introduce myself to myself and develop a beautiful and loving relationship. There's a beautiful and loving person stepping out into the world.

♥

Allergies

Looking back over my life I realized that I was suffering from allergies. My environment and diet caused me to sneeze and experience a nasal drip. This allergy was not physical but spiritual. I allowed myself to react to the external by focusing too much on those things I couldn't control. Eating from the table of worry caused my body to over react. A spiritual cleansing was needed which consisted of letting go of old thoughts and behaviors. It was necessary to change my diet by eating from the table of peace and calmness and allowing myself to be still.

♥

Solid, Liquid, Gas

The Universe helped me to see that it was important for me to be like solid, liquid, or gas. Learning how to be different consistencies at different times in my life is necessary for my growth. Being solid helps me to stand on the truth and not waiver. As a liquid I can flow with life instead of resisting it. By being in a gas form it's easier for me to float and move as the Spirit would move me. There are times where I will be in more than one form at a time but no matter how the Universe guides me I am willing to follow my path.

Sticky Traps

When our minds are open to things that are not conducive for our growth such as a lack of love for oneself, we can be like glue traps. These traps are used to catch rodents, but also attract bugs, insects, dust, and dirt. How can we really see ourselves and grow when we have so much stuff stuck to our minds. When we learn to focus on what's important we get rid of those sticky traps, which causes blockages.

♥

Sweat

Why am I sweating, emitting, and excreting body fluids when I don't have to? I've been perspiring and getting wet for no reason. I have the ability to cool myself off and regulate my own body temperature. I don't have to allow my precious body fluids to flow when it doesn't have to by over working myself internally. The Universe is teaching me not to sweat and allow the heat on the outside to change my body temperature on the inside.

♥

The Assassin

Some experiences in life are like assassins that are hired to kill. I've experienced an assassin coming into my life and killing the poor me attitude. This assassin killed what I couldn't use. Poor me was a prominent and powerful political figure in my world that ruled with great force. The assassin killed poor me for payment of freeing myself. When poor me died, it was disposed of immediately. There was no need for a funeral, memorial, or visitors.

Pin the Tail On the Donkey

In this game (which is usually played by children at birthday parties) a child is blindfolded, turned around and is sent in the direction of a picture of a donkey on the wall. Now the child must pin a tail on the donkey. Now there are different characters used with different objects to pin on but its still the same game. Spirit said we've had things pinned on us from the past and childhood. We reaffirm these incidents by pinning them onto ourselves. As children we weren't aware of the conditioning that was taking place, this was the process of blindfolding us. As we become more aware of the Divine within we can take off the blindfold and stop pinning things on ourselves. There is room for forgiving others and forgiving ourselves.

♥

Don't Stick Me With The Bill

So often we come in contact with people and situations that uses up our energy unnecessarily. The energy we give to others leaves us depleted and someone or something else energized. This is like going out to eat with someone that always sticks you with the bill and leaves. Not only will this person eat his or her food but will eat yours also. An important lesson to learn is that we don't have to be depleted and not give to ourselves. The Universe will show us how, when, where, and whom to give to.

♥

Battery Operated And Remote Controlled

Past memories can control us with words and experiences that occurred a long time ago. The energy of the words that were used is like a battery that was placed in us that keeps us reacting and hurting unnecessarily. The remote control is being used when we listen to what someone else said rather than what the Universe is telling us. Just because someone said something doesn't make what was said true. The Universe encourages self-love and anything that doesn't support self-love must be released.

Set The Bomb Off

Spirit has set off a bomb to kill all pests and anything that is unhealthy for me.

When there are roaches in a house they can come in through different ways. Sometimes the house is not clean and roaches are attracted to food or old things that are left piled up. Even boxes and junk that needs to be thrown out attracts roaches because they like to live in hidden places. There are also times that we may go to someone else's home that has roaches, they may get into our bags or on our coats, and we go home with them. Other times we may come into contact with them in public places and some how they may get into our belongings. Once they are in our homes they begin to multiply quickly and not always easy to get rid of. This also happens to us spiritually. They get into our atmosphere and affect the way we live. Roaches crawl over things we use in the kitchen and if we're not careful into containers that we use for food. This also happens in the bathroom. We see the signs that they are around by the droppings and stains they leave behind. Sometimes we attract roaches because we are in a place mentally or physically that causes the roaches to come to us. After a while there are so many of them that they cause blockages unless we get rid of them.

Sometimes we have to set off a spiritual bomb, which is the truth that helps us to see that our homes are infested with roaches, people, thoughts, and behaviors that we can't use. The truth is so strong that it causes us to come out of our homes to really see what is going on. It then allows us to go back in and clean up what we can't use so that we can move forward.

MOVING FORWARD

As I moved forward in life no one else knew about the eruptions, commotions, convulsions, seizures and disruptions but me.

MOVING FORWARD

You don't have to be perfect. Just be yourself and go with the flow of life; be flexible. Change your form whenever it is needed to mix with the flow.

♥

Take a giant leap forward and fly. See yourself like a balloon that has just been released. There are no strings attached and you've ascended on high. The only way you'll come down is if you deflate yourself.

♥

You don't have to be on the assembly line of life and continue to be pre-packaged with someone else's wrappings and coverings. These wrappings, plastic, and coverings have been taken off so you and I can breathe. We are exposed and don't have to worry about spoiling and going into a refrigerator or freezer. There is no more expiration date to determine our freshness. We don't have to live a shelf life.

♥

The Creator will show us the secret place and the pavilion (a place of peace) when we are still. This province is inside all of us. It is a peaceful place that gives us the answers, courage, and strength we need to move forward.

♥

As I moved forward in life no one else knew about the eruptions, commotions, convulsions, seizures, and disruptions but me. When I learned to take my shoes off and stand on holy ground—peace and calmness came upon me and said, "Be still, stand still and know that I am God."

♥

Be in the company of people who see the = sign instead of greater than >
or less than <. When we are involved in greater than or less than relationships, others are gaining our energy and we are left drained. When we are
equal in our relationships, there are opportunities for both of us to be
strengthened and encouraged. We can respect each other.

Are you playing Simon Says or red light, green light, 1,2,3? Ask yourself
this question, "Am I letting someone or something else control my life?"
Take the necessary steps to empower yourself so you can play the game of
life and have more fun.

Are you depending on external things as your source, such as people and
what they say or do? Consider the times you got through some really
rough spots. Also recall the times that you may have cried by yourself and
when you let it out, you learned to let go and the answers came to you.
Right now your source is the Universe.

It's time to stop having tantrums and overreacting when natural changes
occur. It's time to grow up. How can we effectively help or touch others
when we can't control ourselves? There are some things we have to put
away and get rid of. We can't act the way we did fifteen years ago, today.
Be rooted in the truth, not in limited thinking. When we launch into the
deep, which are new areas of understanding and experiences in our lives,
we won't explode and disintegrate during our flight. We will know what
it's like to fly.

Look at every nook and cranny in your life to see what's been hidden. See
how you've been really acting. Enforce your tamper-resistant seal through
the truth, from lessons learned, and knowing yourself. The octopuses'

arms will become clearer when you realize that they are the people, places, and things that have been squeezing the life out of you all this time.

Every time you allow someone or something else to take your attention and lead you, there is conflict. Some people become complacent and accept someone or something else controlling their lives. This brings so many disharmonies, which causes warring and fighting within us. You may want and keep asking people to understand where you're coming from, but first you have to understand where you're coming from and where you're going.

♥

Honor and listen to yourself. Often we give out so much we don't always take the time to look within. Come out from your distractions, whatever it is or whoever it is and step back. Pay attention to what's inside of you.

♥

The process of life will not fight with you. It's better to accept and take on the responsibility that's before you. Your life is more than you think. There are lessons for us to learn. These lessons are more important than people, places, or things that you've experienced.

♥

Sometimes we stop trusting what we know and take our eyes off of our goals. When we start to look around everything becomes magnified and distracts us. This is a reminder to get focused again and trust the Universe.

♥

When you listen to your inner voice, which is the Universe speaking, you will learn not to get easily distracted. Distraction causes a back flow in energy and it needs to be released. Things get backed up or caked on and the plunger of truth is needed to clear us.

♥

Pay more attention to the Universe. Sometimes it may feel like you're not hearing correctly and falling apart but in reality you are coming back together.

You are like a diamond, beautiful, and sparkling. Your strength is deeper than you realize. You're like a well, so that the deeper you go the more there is to you. You're really stronger than you think and you can handle whatever comes your way.

♥

All the answers and healing you need are deep within you.

♥

Sometimes we are tested in-house, through personal experiences that others don't know about. When we go out and people and situations start to prod, poke, pull, and pinch we won't fall apart. You must be inspected through various experiences. Products may be pulled, looked over, and go through a process for approval to be sent out for public use. How could you effectively reach anyone else if you can't relate to that person?

♥

We need time and space for ourselves. Let go of the past live right now. We will be lighter when we let go of the heaviness of the past.

♥

We don't have to be so thick and concentrated but be open and mix with water for a better flow of life. Stretch out and see what life has to offer.

♥

When was the last time you took time for yourself? How long has it been? Perhaps it has been too long since you've had quality time. It's been so long since we've really had hugs, touches, and caresses. It's not possible for us to do everything for everyone else and neglect ourselves.

♥

Consistency doesn't mean we're at the same level all the time; but by continuously loving and working on ourselves, we take leaps forward towards making our dreams and desires come true.

♥

Live in the now! Release the past and don't worry about the future. So far the two most powerful things that have affected my life are living in the now and all the power and answers I need are inside; I just have to access them.

♥

Since it's right now, I am learning to bounce back much faster when situations are stressful. Since it's right now, I will release people, places, and things. Since it's right now, I will love and approve of myself. I will run back to my base knowing that God is my source. Right now is so great because I am releasing the various emotions that have been roaming inside for so long. I am learning different ways to build myself up and be at peace.

I taste, smell, see, hear, feel and sense the goodness of the Creator in my life everyday. I'm grateful for my life and what I have right now. The process of life is wonderful. That which I've been seeking is right in front of me. What I think is, is not and what I think is not, is. It's not what I think, it's what I know and the same is true for you.

♥

Things are not always as they seem. Sometimes what we see are mirages because of what we're feeling. It seems like something is in front of us when it actually isn't. Feelings can sometimes cause us to see illusions.

When we learn to see ourselves as the Universe sees us, our vision becomes crystal clear.

♥

Recently I resigned from a job that was not uplifting, meeting my needs, or satisfying. The thought was floating around in my mind to leave and I played with this idea. Even though there were glaring signs telling me to leave I had not made up my mind. One evening I heard Spirit say, "Every time you go to work you are going to a wake. You keep viewing a dead body. This is a dead body that can't be resuscitated. It's time to have the funeral, bury the body, and move on." There was no need to argue and since I wasn't dependent on this job I left that same week and have absolutely no regrets.

♥

The Universe dared me to take on the challenges I face or think I'm facing. Some of the obstacles before me are the ones I created in my own mind.

♥

I am free. Whatever is bound on earth shall be bound in heaven—whatever is loosed on earth shall be loosed in heaven. Heaven and earth are in me. I am free to focus on myself, healing, releasing, letting go and doing what I like to do. All this time I tried to get away from this. It didn't seem right not to do what I've been told all my life. It's more important that I fulfill my purpose and calling. I am constantly learning to let go of every single idea, thought, habit, and feeling that is not conducive to my evolution. I am blessed from all angles, sides, and positions, and these blessings are there for you as well.

♥

I am on the most wanted list to live life to the fullest. Therefore there is no more need for camouflage, disguises, or costumes. It's right now. The past is over and done.

♥

Aim for the big things. We can get rid of the compact size. You are going from a pinhole to wide angle. It's time to let the light come in and see things bigger and better. Don't let the fear of success frighten you. Accept and embrace it. It belongs to you.

AFFIRMATIONS FOR YOUR JOURNEY

I am protected where I go.

I love and approve of myself.

I am getting better everyday.

The Universe within will lead and guide me into all truth.

I deserve the best.

The Universe will supply all my needs.

All things work together for my good.

I let go of the old and allow the new to come in.

I accept myself just as I am.

I am willing to change.

All is well in my world.

I listen to the Universe within.

I hear the voice of God and follow my intuitive leads.

I am never alone.

My needs are always taken care of.

When I follow the Divine Design for my life the desires of my heart come to pass.

IT'S RIGHT NOW

When I say it's right now this releases me of the
infirmities from my mother's womb and beyond.

When I say it's right now I enter a place of peace.

When I say it's right now I let go of myself and dare to do
all the things my mind says I can do.

When I say it's right now, the fragments of my life
that were scattered in the wind come back
together and unite in strength and love.

When I say it's right now I am no longer afraid.

When I live in the now, I am free.

© 2003 by Dawn A. Bruce

978-0-595-47188

0-595-47188-9

Printed in the United States
201959BV00003B/508-531/A

9 780595 471881